Machines to the Rescue

Tow Trucks

by Bizzy Harris

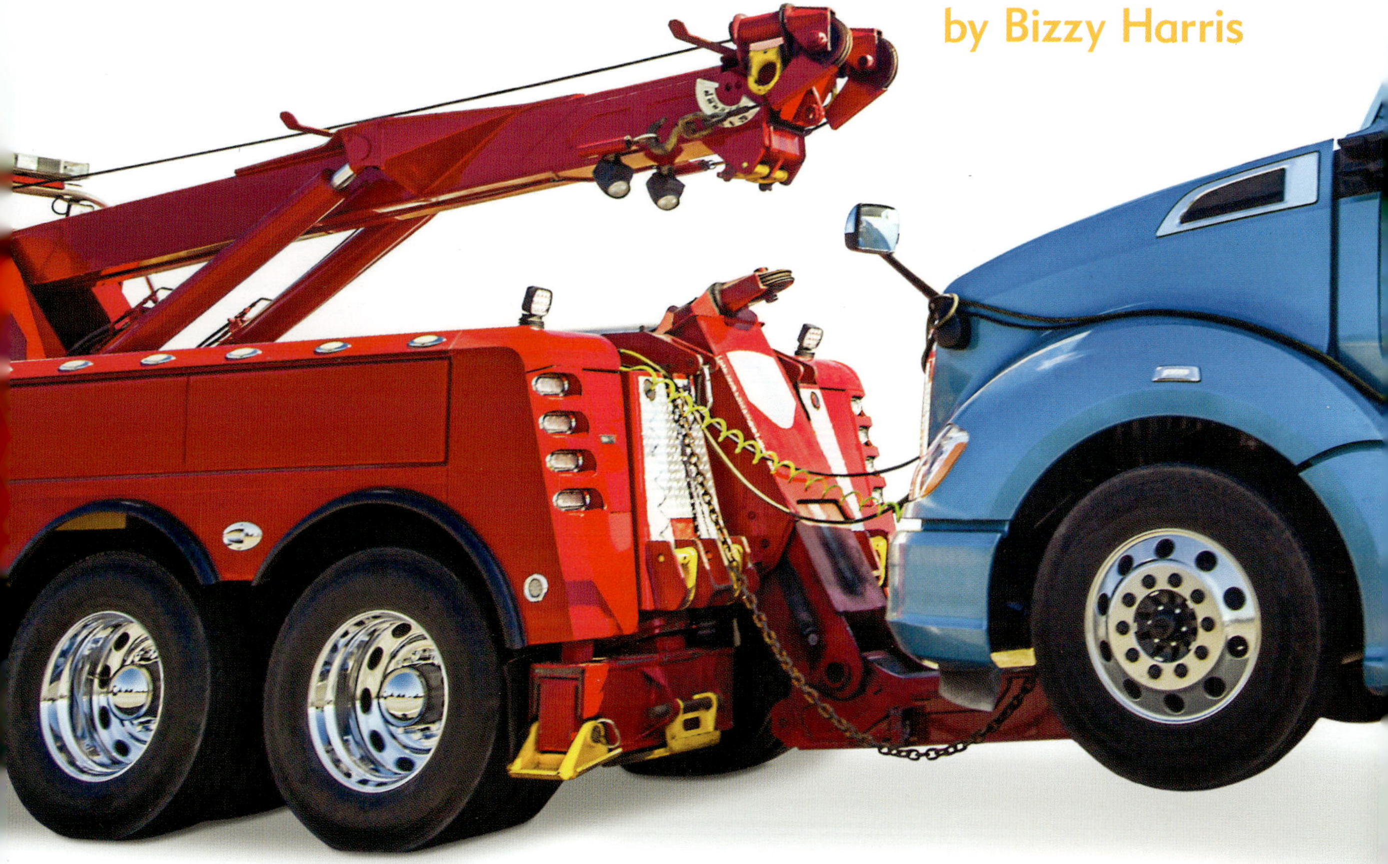

Ideas for Parents and Teachers

Bullfrog Books let children practice reading informational text at the earliest reading levels. Repetition, familiar words, and photo labels support early readers.

Before Reading

- Discuss the cover photo. What does it tell them?
- Look at the picture glossary together. Read and discuss the words.

Read the Book

- "Walk" through the book and look at the photos. Let the child ask questions. Point out the photo labels.
- Read the book to the child, or have him or her read independently.

After Reading

- Prompt the child to think more. Ask: Have you ever seen a tow truck? What was it towing?

Bullfrog Books are published by Jump!
5357 Penn Avenue South
Minneapolis, MN 55419
www.jumplibrary.com

Library of Congress Cataloging-in-Publication Data

Names: Harris, Bizzy, author.
Title: Tow trucks / by Bizzy Harris.
Description: Minneapolis, MN: Jump!, Inc. [2022]
Series: Machines to the rescue | Includes index.
Audience: Ages 5–8. | Audience: Grades K–1.
Identifiers: LCCN 2020041858 (print)
LCCN 2020041859 (ebook)
ISBN 9781645279228 (hardcover)
ISBN 9781645279235 (paperback)
ISBN 9781645279242 (ebook)
Subjects: LCSH: Wreckers (Vehicles)—Juvenile literature.
Classification: LCC TL230.5.W74 H37 2022 (print)
LCC TL230.5.W74 (ebook) | DDC 629.225—dc23
LC record available at https://lccn.loc.gov/2020041858
LC ebook record available at https://lccn.loc.gov/2020041859

Editor: Jenna Gleisner
Designer: Molly Ballanger

Photo Credits: kozmoat98/iStock, cover; Siegfried Schnepf/iStock, 1; gpflman/iStock, 3, 22mr; IPGGutenbergUKLtd/iStock, 4; Andyqwe/iStock, 5; Eva-christiane Wilm/Dreamstime, 6, 23tl; ITisha/Shutterstock, 6–7, 9, 23bl; Thinkstock/Getty, 8, 23tr; ThamKC/Shutterstock, 10–11; PBWPIX/Alamy, 12–13; mikedabell/iStock, 14–15; Kunal Mehta/Shutterstock, 16; Vibrant Image Studio/Shutterstock, 17; Cavan/Alamy, 18–19, 20–21; Art Konovalov/Shutterstock, 22t; Miwi97/Dreamstime, 22b; rzelich/iStock, 22ml; algre/Shutterstock, 23br; Volodymyr Krasyuk/Shutterstock, 24.

Printed in the United States of America at Corporate Graphics in North Mankato, Minnesota.

Table of Contents

Lift and Tow 4
Types of Tow Trucks 22
Picture Glossary 23
Index 24
To Learn More 24

Lift and Tow

Oh, no!

A car broke down.

What can help?

A tow truck!

The driver uses controls.

They move parts of the truck.

control

They move a pulley.

It pulls a vehicle up the ramp.
ramp

strap

The driver puts straps on the wheels.

They keep the car in place.

It can’t roll off the ramp.

This tow truck
pulls a vehicle.

It lifts the
back wheels.

They don't touch
the ground.

This tow truck lifts a whole car.

Cool!

Some tow trucks carry many cars.

Some carry big machines.

Wow!

This truck went off the road.
A tow truck helps!

It pulls the truck out.

Now it can get fixed.

Thank you!

Types of Tow Trucks

There are many kinds of tow trucks. Take a look at some!

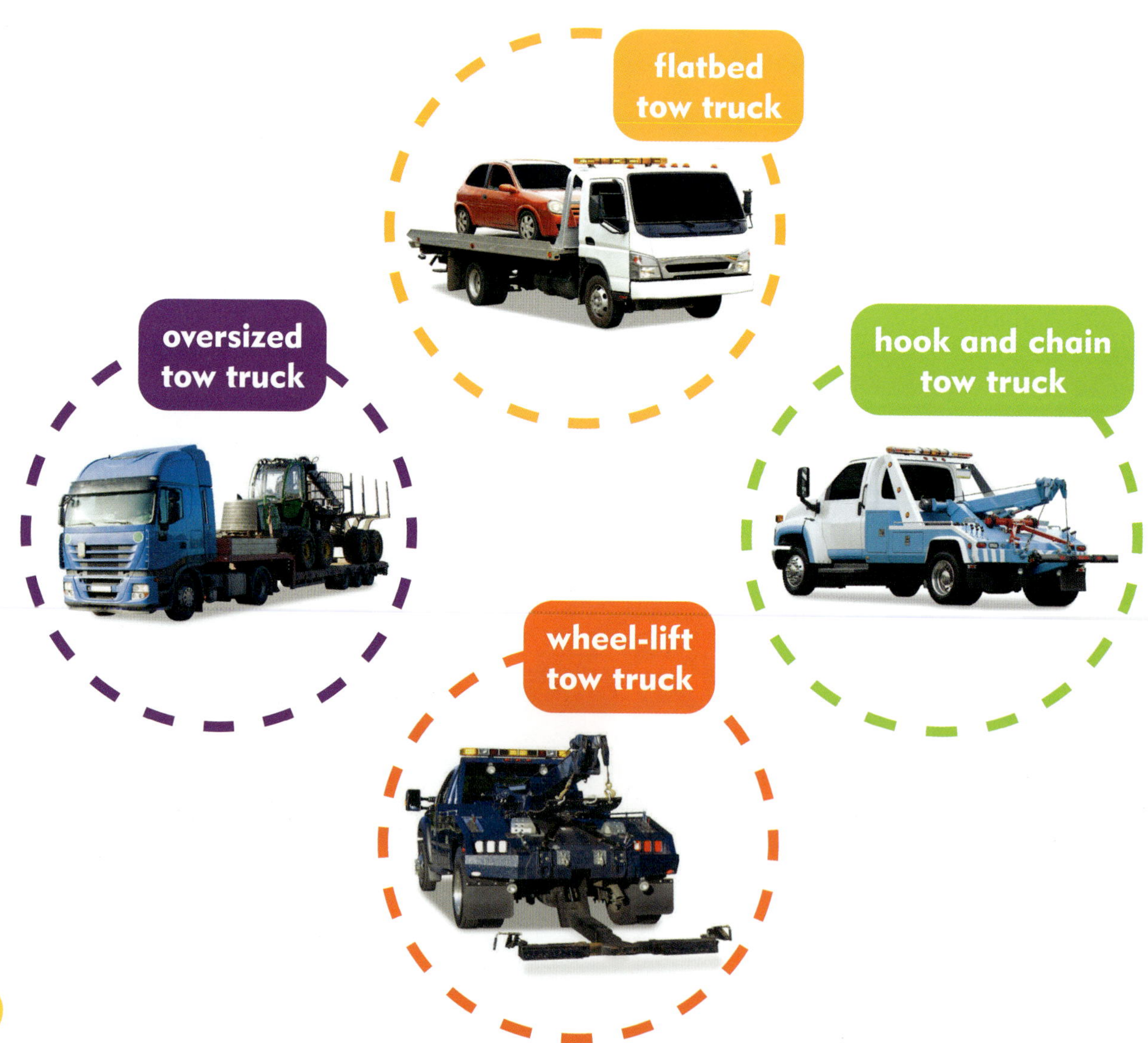

Picture Glossary

controls
Devices used to operate machines.

pulley
A wheel over which a rope or chain is pulled to lift or lower an object.

ramp
A sloping platform that links one level with another.

vehicle
A machine, such as a car, truck, or van, that is used to transport people or goods.

Index

carry 16, 17
controls 6
driver 6, 11
help 5, 19
lifts 12, 15
machines 17
pulley 8
pulls 9, 12, 20
ramp 9, 11
road 19
straps 11
wheels 11, 12

To Learn More

Finding more information is as easy as 1, 2, 3.

1. Go to www.factsurfer.com
2. Enter "towtrucks" into the search box.
3. Choose your book to see a list of websites.